Piano Duet PLAY-ALONG

VOLUME 36

HOLIDAY FAVORITES

ISBN 978-1-4234-8011-2

HAL•LEONARD® CORPORATION

7777 W. BLUEMOUND RD. P.O. BOX 13819 MILWAUKEE, WI 53213

Visit Hal Leonard Online at
www.halleonard.com

CONTENTS

DO YOU HEAR WHAT I HEAR

SECONDO

Words and Music by NOEL REGNEY
and GLORIA SHAYNE

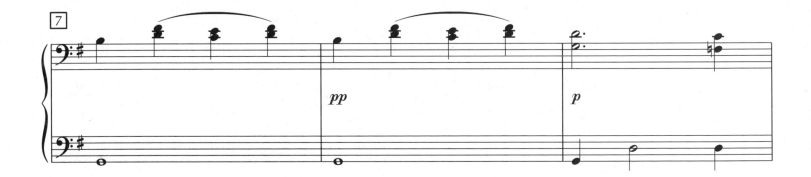

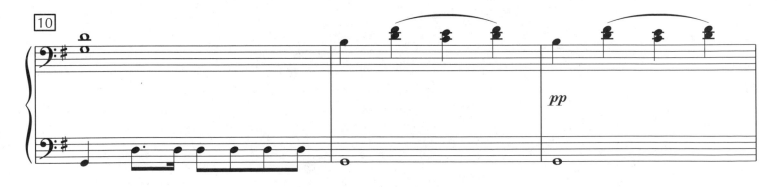

DO YOU HEAR WHAT I HEAR

PRIMO

Words and Music by NOEL REGNEY
and GLORIA SHAYNE

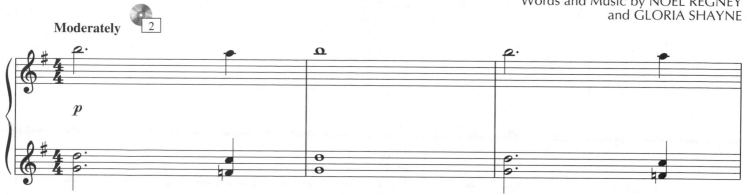

PRIMO

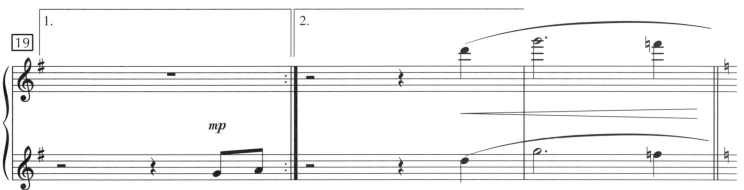

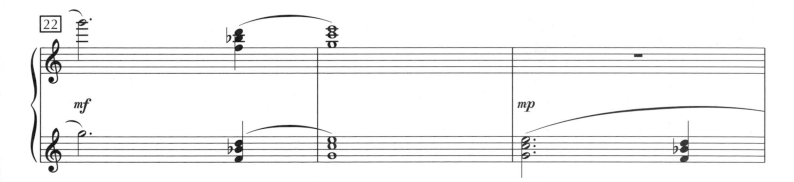

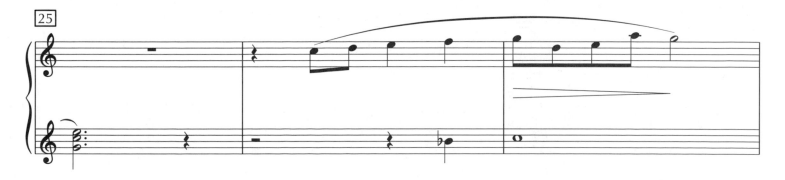

SECONDO

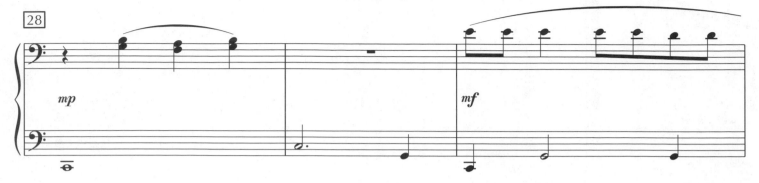

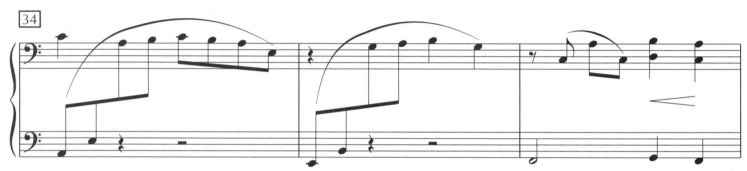

PRIMO

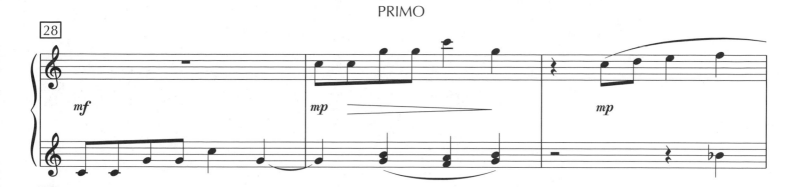

FROSTY THE SNOW MAN

SECONDO

Words and Music by STEVE NELSON
and JACK ROLLINS

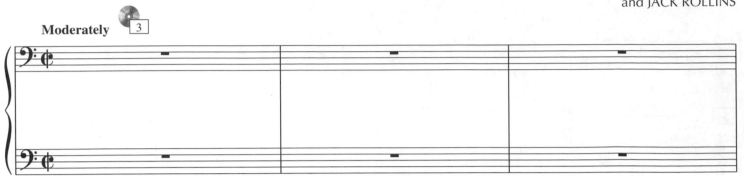

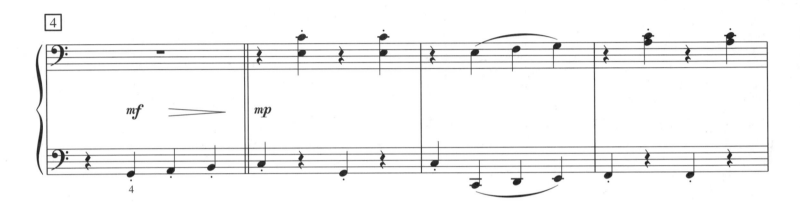

FROSTY THE SNOW MAN

PRIMO

Words and Music by STEVE NELSON
and JACK ROLLINS

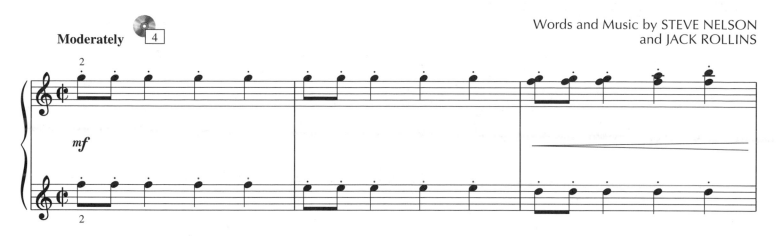

SECONDO

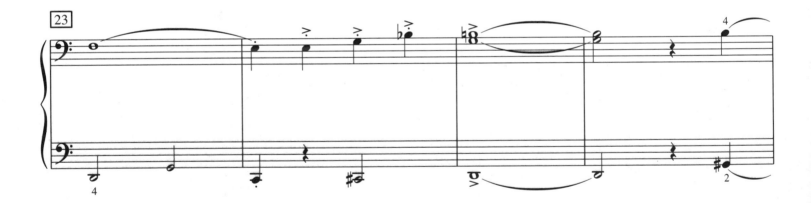

PRIMO

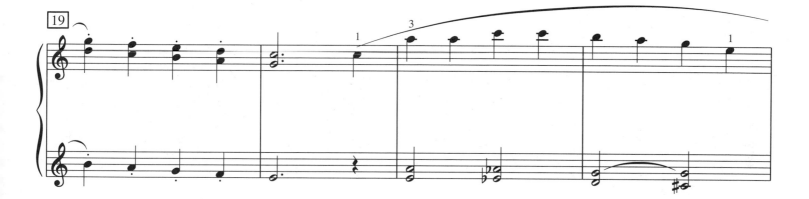

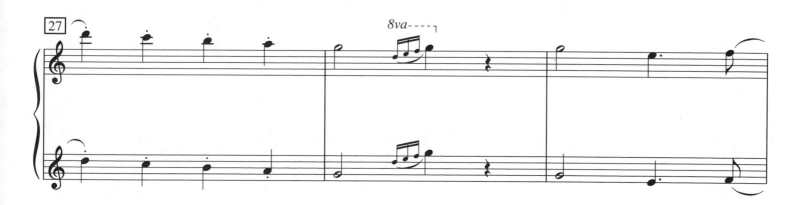

SECONDO

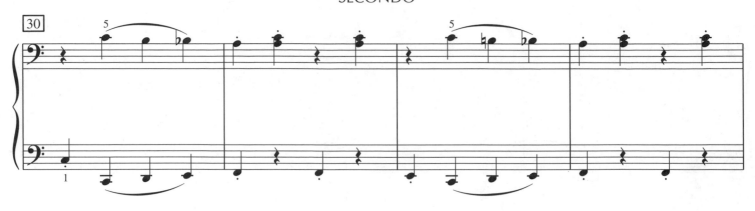

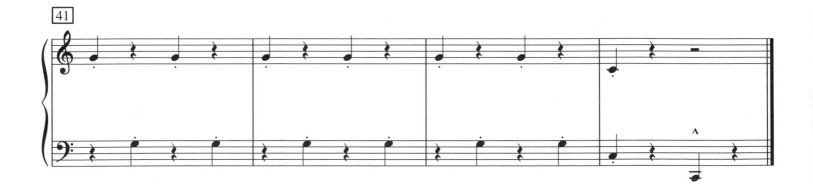

PRIMO

HERE COMES SANTA CLAUS
(Right Down Santa Claus Lane)

SECONDO

Words and Music by GENE AUTRY
and OAKLEY HALDEMAN

With a bounce

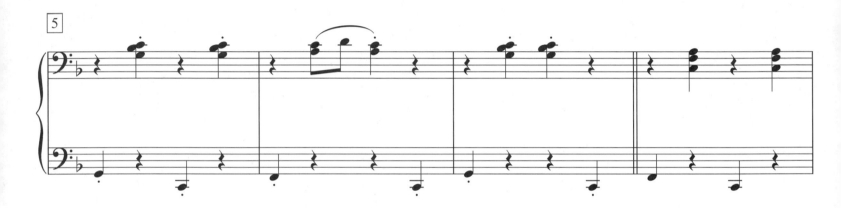

HERE COMES SANTA CLAUS
(Right Down Santa Claus Lane)

PRIMO

Words and Music by GENE AUTRY
and OAKLEY HALDEMAN

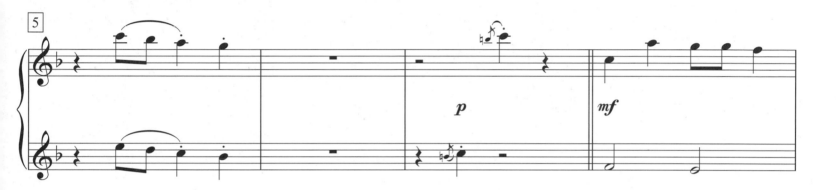

SECONDO

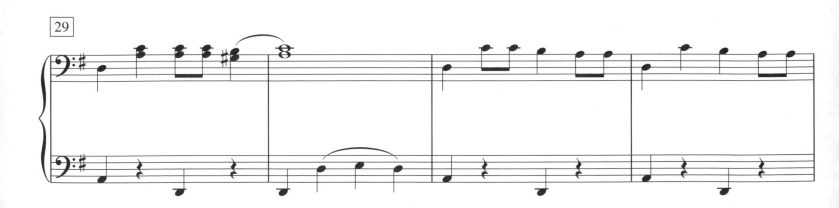

PRIMO

SECONDO

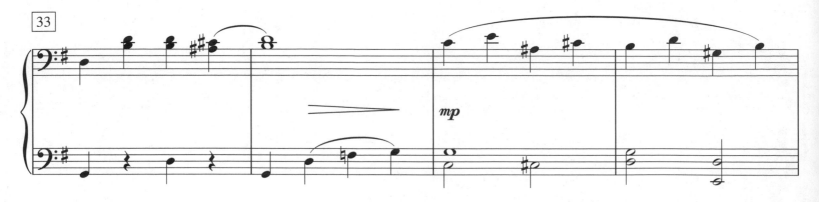

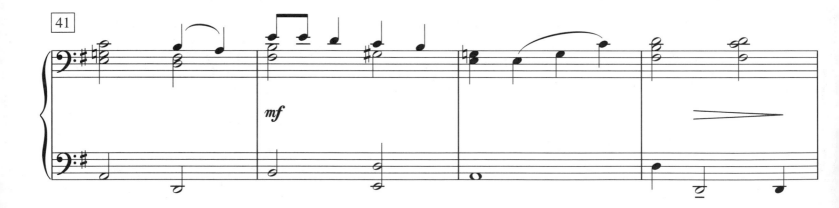

PRIMO

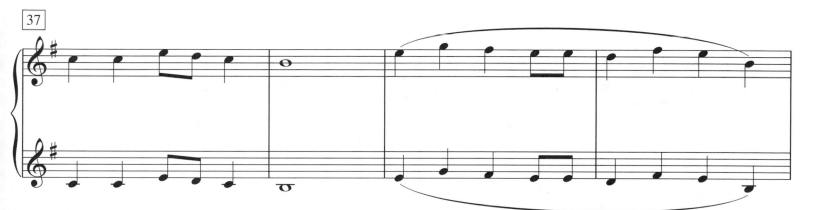

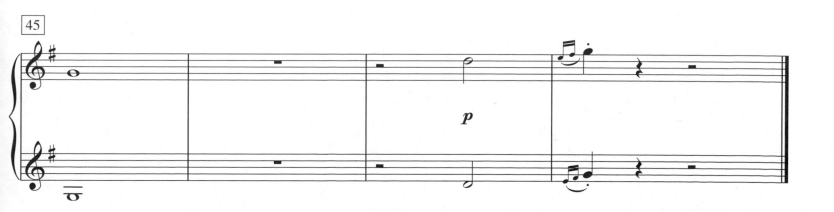

(There's No Place Like)
HOME FOR THE HOLIDAYS

SECONDO

Words by AL STILLMAN
Music by ROBERT ALLEN

Moderately, with expression

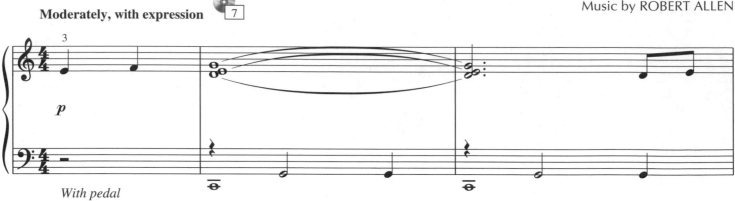

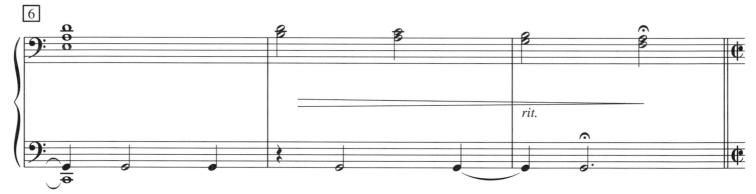

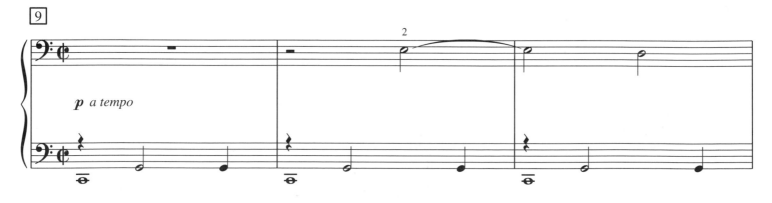

(There's No Place Like)
HOME FOR THE HOLIDAYS

PRIMO

Words by AL STILLMAN
Music by ROBERT ALLEN

SECONDO

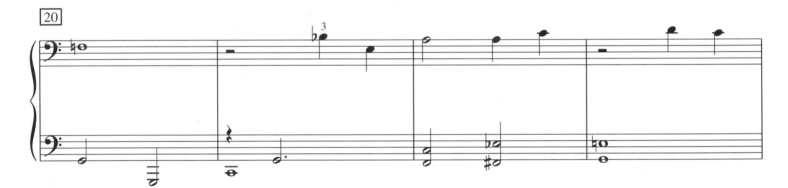

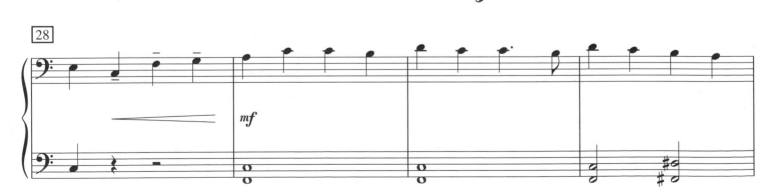

PRIMO

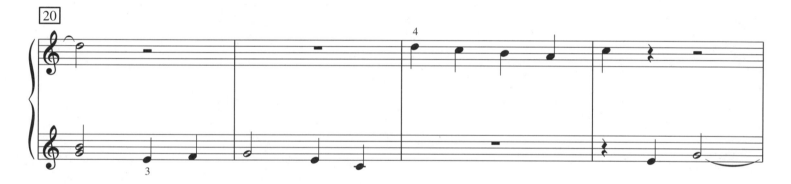

SECONDO

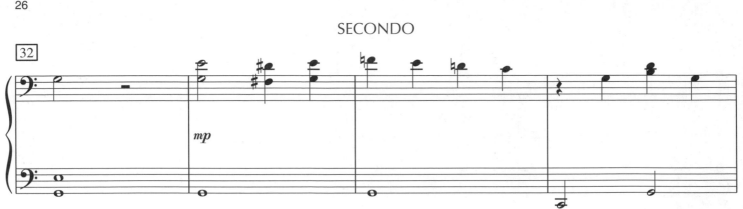

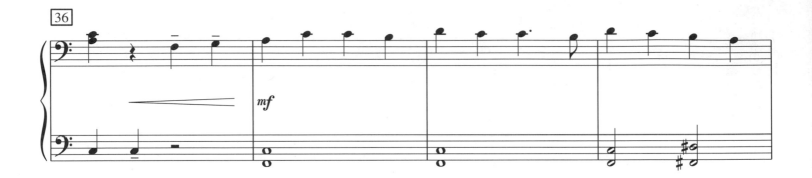

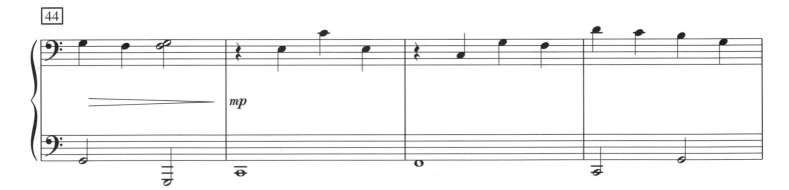

PRIMO

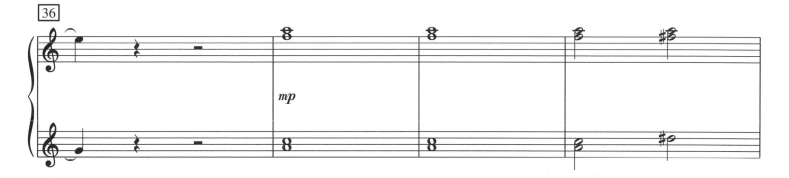

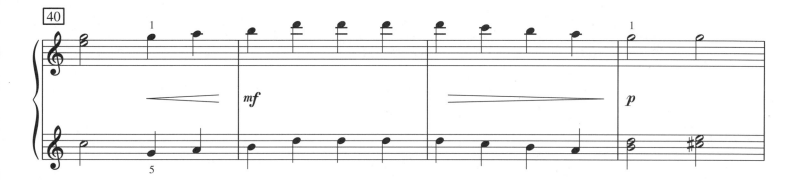

SECONDO

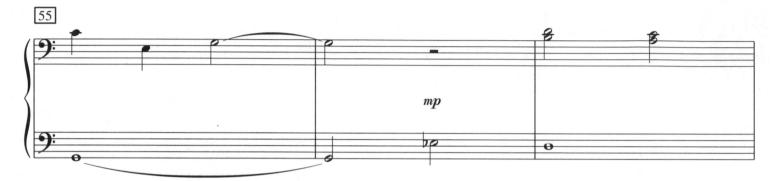

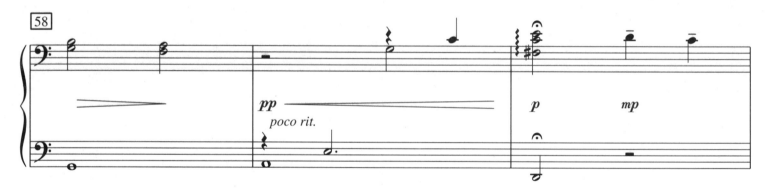

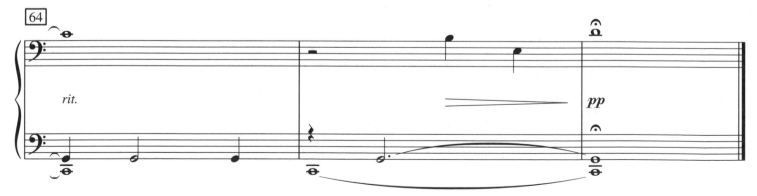

PRIMO

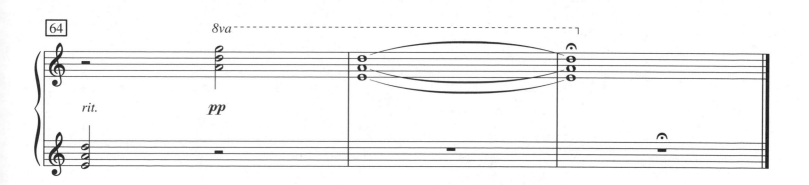

I SAW MOMMY KISSING SANTA CLAUS

SECONDO

Words and Music by
TOMMIE CONNOR

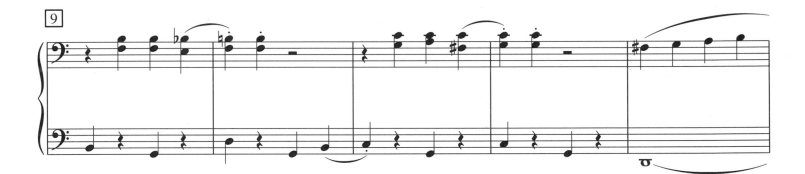

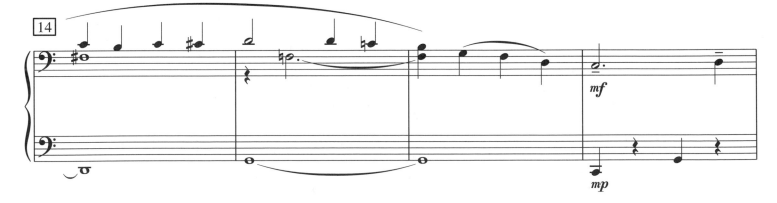

I SAW MOMMY KISSING SANTA CLAUS

PRIMO

Words and Music by
TOMMIE CONNOR

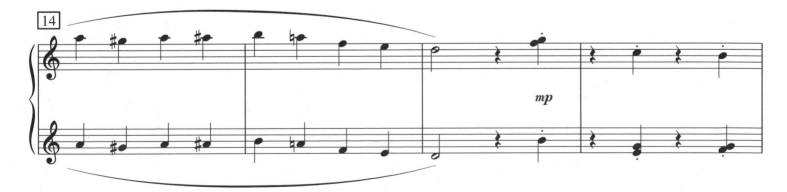

SECONDO

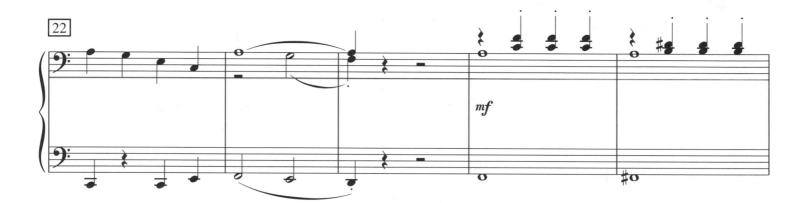

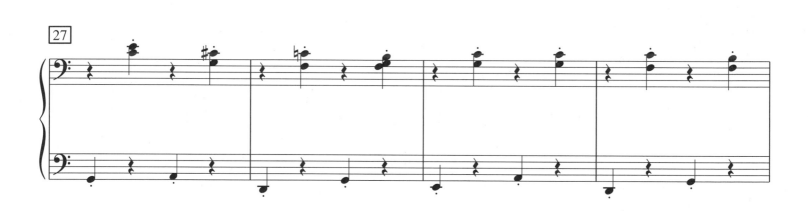

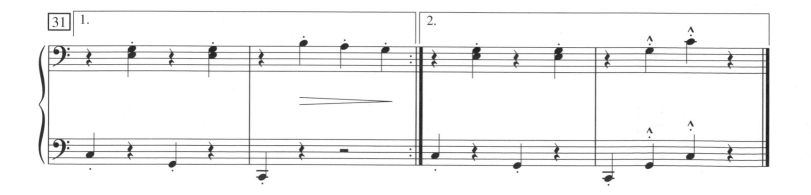

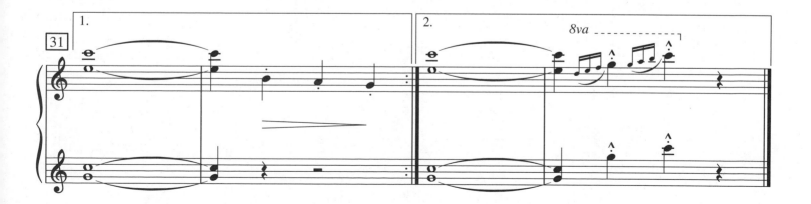

JINGLE-BELL ROCK

SECONDO

Words and Music by JOE BEAL
and JIM BOOTHE

JINGLE-BELL ROCK

PRIMO

Words and Music by JOE BEAL
and JIM BOOTHE

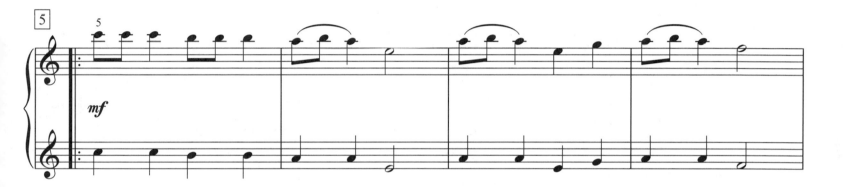

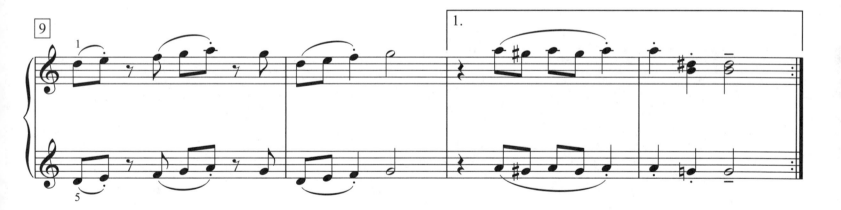

SECONDO

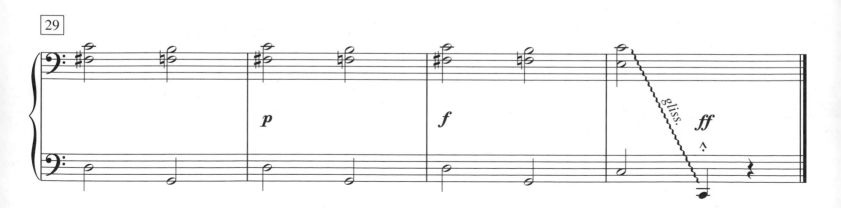

LET IT SNOW! LET IT SNOW! LET IT SNOW!

SECONDO

Words by SAMMY CAHN
Music by JULE STYNE

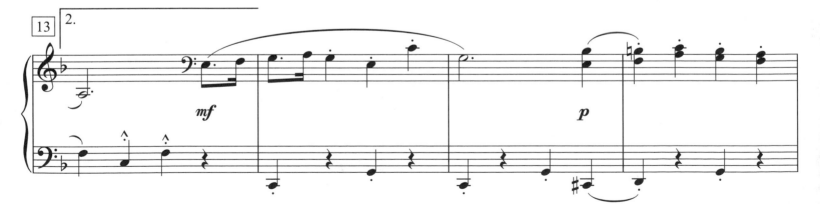

LET IT SNOW! LET IT SNOW! LET IT SNOW!

PRIMO

Words by SAMMY CAHN
Music by JULE STYNE

With a lilt, not too fast

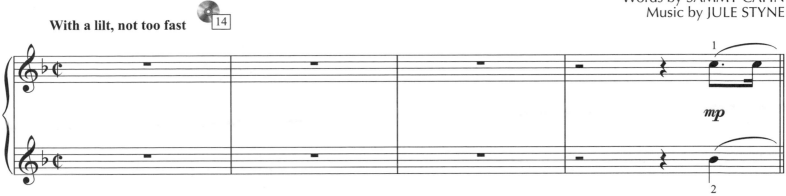

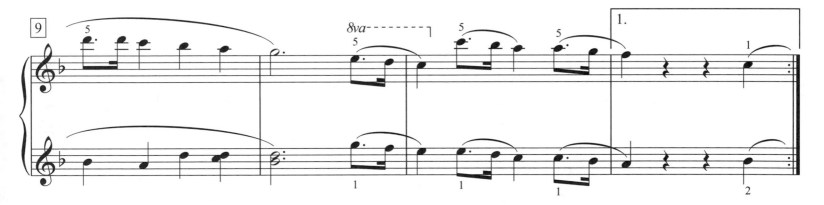

SECONDO

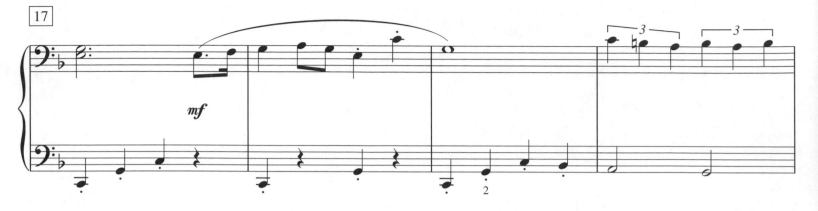

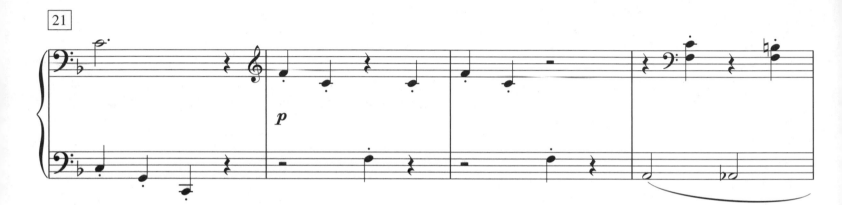

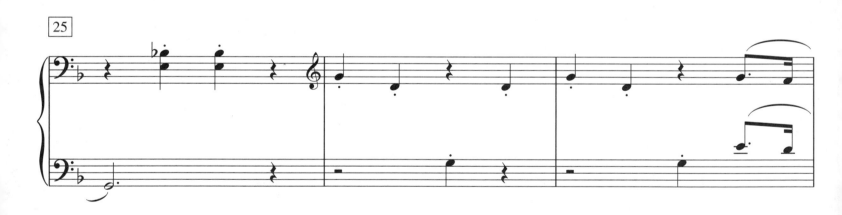

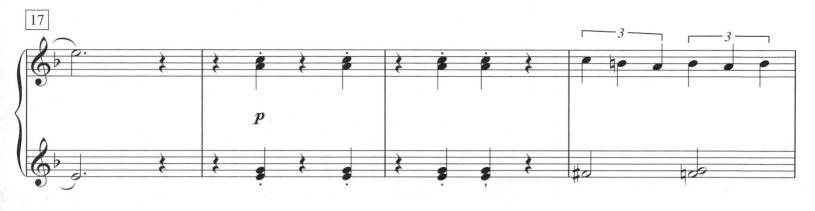

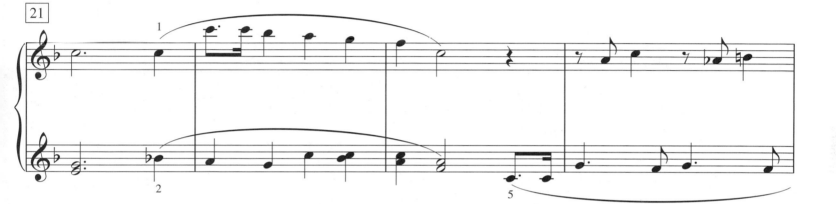

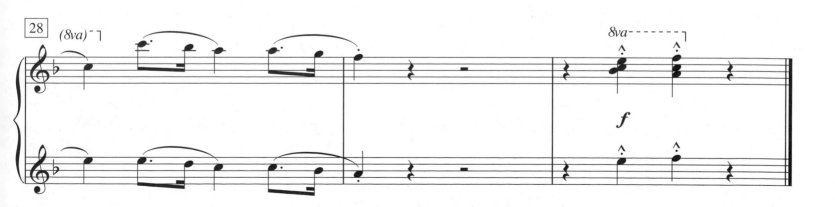

LITTLE SAINT NICK

SECONDO

Words and Music by BRIAN WILSON
and MIKE LOVE

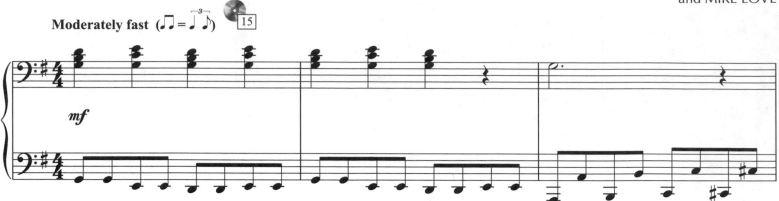

LITTLE SAINT NICK

PRIMO

Words and Music by BRIAN WILSON
and MIKE LOVE

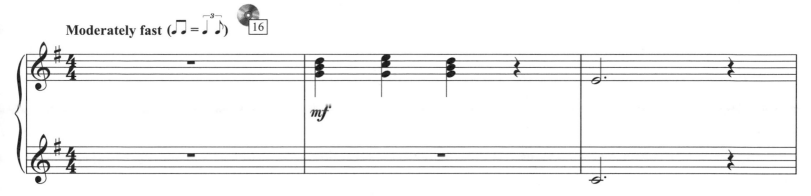

SECONDO

PRIMO

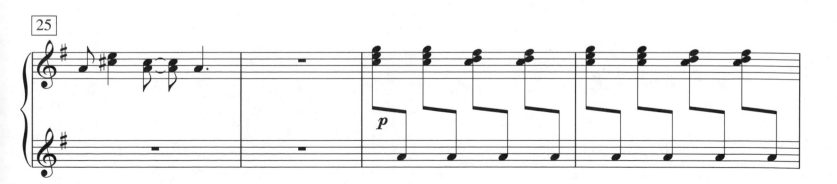

SECONDO

MERRY CHRISTMAS, DARLING

SECONDO

Words and Music by RICHARD CARPENTER
and FRANK POOLER

MERRY CHRISTMAS, DARLING

PRIMO

Words and Music by RICHARD CARPENTER
and FRANK POOLER

With expression

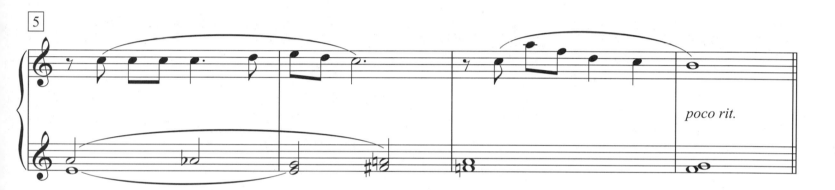

Moderately slow

PRIMO

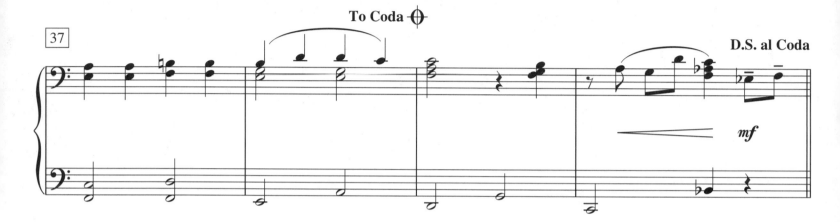

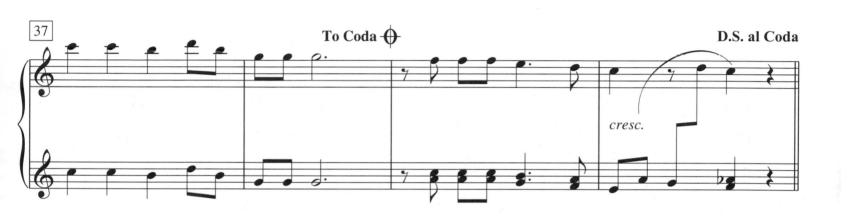

SANTA CLAUS IS COMIN' TO TOWN

SECONDO

Words by HAVEN GILLESPIE
Music by J. FRED COOTS

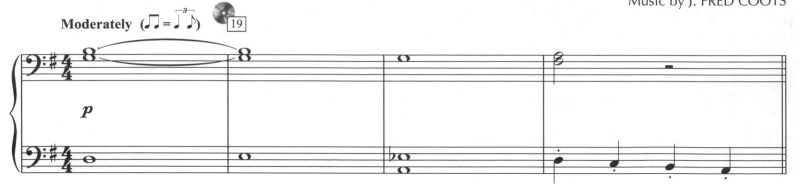

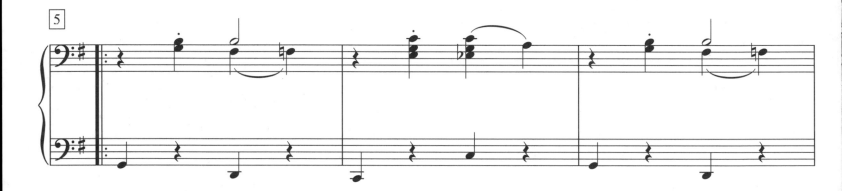

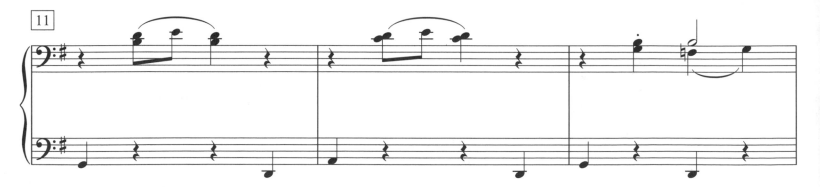

SANTA CLAUS IS COMIN' TO TOWN

PRIMO

Words by HAVEN GILLESPIE
Music by J. FRED COOTS

SECONDO

PRIMO

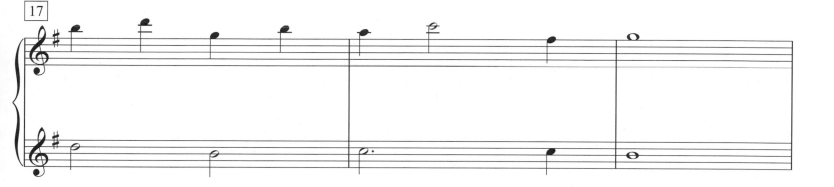

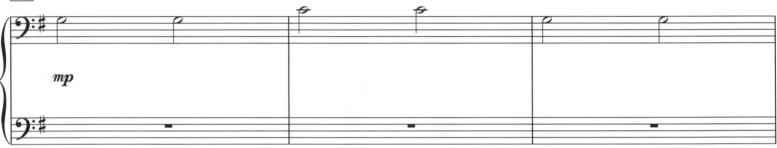

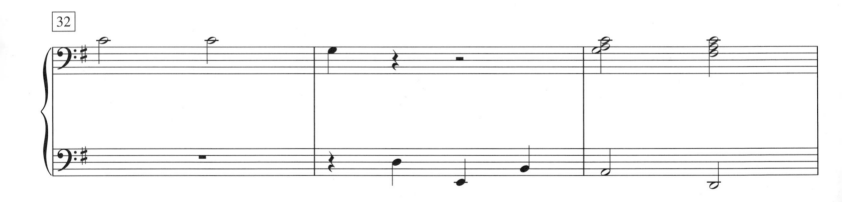

PRIMO

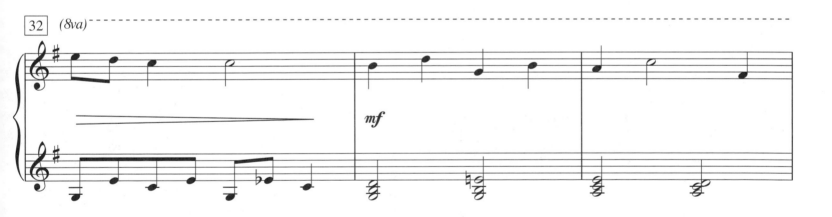

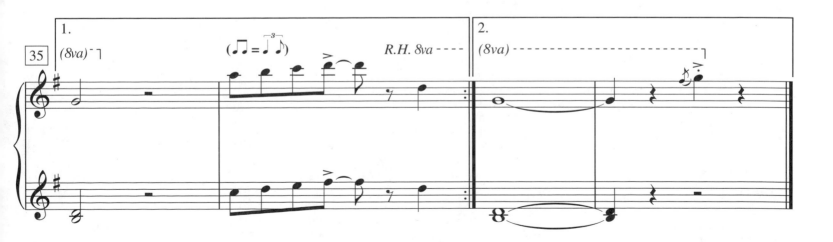

CELEBRATE THE SEASON

with Christmas Songbooks for Piano from Hal Leonard

17 Super Christmas Hits

This book contains the most popular, most requested Christmas titles: The Christmas Song • Frosty the Snow Man • A Holly Jolly Christmas • Home for the Holidays • I'll Be Home for Christmas • It's Beginning to Look like Christmas • Jingle-Bell Rock • Let It Snow! Let It Snow! Let It Snow! • The Little Drummer Boy • Mister Santa • Sleigh Ride • We Need a Little Christmas • and more.
00240867 Big-Note Piano $9.95
00361053 Easy Piano $9.95

25 Top Christmas Songs

Includes: Blue Christmas • C-H-R-I-S-T-M-A-S • The Christmas Song • The Christmas Waltz • Do You Hear What I Hear • Have Yourself a Merry Little Christmas • Here Comes Santa Claus • Jingle-Bell Rock • Last Christmas • Pretty Paper • Silver Bells • and more.
00490058 Easy Piano $11.95

Best Christmas Music

A giant collection of 62 Christmas favorites: Away in a Manger • Blue Christmas • The Chipmunk Song • The First Noel • Frosty the Snow Man • Grandma Got Run Over by a Reindeer • I Saw Mommy Kissing Santa Claus • Pretty Paper • Silver Bells • Wonderful Christmastime • more.
00310325 Big-Note Piano $14.95

The Best Christmas Songs Ever

A treasured collection of 70 songs: The Christmas Song • Frosty the Snow Man • Grandma Got Run Over by a Reindeer • Here Comes Santa Claus • A Holly Jolly Christmas • I'll Be Home for Christmas • Jingle-Bell Rock • Let It Snow! Let It Snow! Let It Snow! • Santa Claus Is Comin' to Town • more!
00364130 Easy Piano $19.95

Children's Christmas Songs

22 holiday favorites, including: Frosty the Snow Man • Jingle Bells • Jolly Old St. Nicholas • Rudolph, the Red-Nosed Reindeer • Up on the Housetop • and more!
00222547 Easy Piano $7.95

Christmas Pops

THE PHILLIP KEVEREN SERIES

18 holiday favorites: Because It's Christmas • Blue Christmas • Christmas Time Is Here • I'll Be Home for Christmas • Mary, Did You Know? • Rockin' Around the Christmas Tree • Silver Bells • Tennessee Christmas • more.
00311126 Easy Piano $12.95

Christmas Songs

12 songs, including: Caroling, Caroling • Christmas Time Is Here • Do You Hear What I Hear • Here Comes Santa Claus • It's Beginning to Look like Christmas • Little Saint Nick • Merry Christmas, Darling • Mistletoe and Holly • and more.
00311242 Easy Piano Solo..........................$8.95

Christmas Traditions

THE PHILLIP KEVEREN SERIES

20 beloved songs arranged for beginning soloists: Away in a Manger • Coventry Carol • Deck the Hall • God Rest Ye Merry, Gentlemen • Jingle Bells • Silent Night • We Three Kings of Orient Are • more.
00311117 Beginning Piano Solos................$10.99

Greatest Christmas Hits

18 Christmas classics: Blue Christmas • Brazilian Sleigh Bells • The Christmas Song • Do You Hear What I Hear • Here Comes Santa Claus • I Saw Mommy Kissing Santa Claus • Silver Bells • This Christmas • more!
00311136 Big-Note Piano $9.95

Jazz Up Your Christmas

ARRANGED BY LEE EVANS

12 Christmas carols in a fresh perspective. Full arrangements may be played as a concert suite. Songs include: Deck the Hall • The First Noel • God Rest Ye Merry Gentlemen • The Holly and the Ivy • O Christmas Tree • What Child Is This? • and more.
00009040 Piano Solo $9.95

Jingle Jazz

THE PHILLIP KEVEREN SERIES

17 Christmas standards: Caroling, Caroling • The Christmas Song • I'll Be Home for Christmas • Jingle Bells • Merry Christmas, Darling • The Most Wonderful Time of the Year • Rudolph the Red-Nosed Reindeer • We Wish You a Merry Christmas • and more.
00310762 Piano Solo $12.95

100 Christmas Carols

Includes the Christmas classics: Angels We Have Heard on High • Bring a Torch, Jeannette Isabella • Dance of the Sugar Plum Fairy • The First Noel • Here We Come A-Wassailing • It Came upon the Midnight Clear • Joy to the World • Still, Still, Still • The Twelve Days of Christmas • We Three Kings of Orient Are • and more!
00311134 Easy Piano.................................$15.95

The Nutcracker Suite

ARRANGED BY BILL BOYD

7 easy piano arrangements from Tchaikovsky's beloved ballet. Includes "Dance of the Sugar-Plum Fairy."
00110010 Easy Piano.................................$8.95

The Ultimate Series: Christmas

The ultimate collection of Christmas classics includes 100 songs: Carol of the Bells • The Chipmunk Song • Christmas Time Is Here • Do You Hear What I Hear • The First Noel • Gesù Bambino • Happy Xmas (War Is Over) • Jesu, Joy of Man's Desiring • Silver and Gold • What Child Is This? • Wonderful Christmastime • and more.
00241003 Easy Piano.................................$19.95

FOR MORE INFORMATION, SEE YOUR LOCAL MUSIC DEALER, OR WRITE TO:

HAL•LEONARD® CORPORATION
7777 W. BLUEMOUND RD. P.O. BOX 13819 MILWAUKEE, WI 53213
Complete songlists online at **www.halleonard.com**

Prices, contents and availability subject to change without notice.

Piano For Two

A VARIETY OF PIANO DUETS FROM HAL LEONARD

LI – THE BEATLES PIANO DUETS – 2ND EDITION
Features 8 arrangements: Can't Buy Me Love • Eleanor Rigby • Hey Jude • Let It Be • Penny Lane • Something • When I'm Sixty-Four • Yesterday.

00290496..$10.95

I – BROADWAY DUETS
9 duet arrangements of Broadway favorites, including: Cabaret • Comedy Tonight • Ol' Man River • One • and more.

00292077 ....$12.99

LI – BROADWAY FAVORITES
A show-stopping collection of 8 songs arranged as piano duets. Includes: I Dreamed a Dream • If Ever I Would Leave You • Memory • People.

00290185 ....$9.95

LI – COLLECTED SACRED CLASSICS
Arranged by Bill Boyd
8 classics for piano duet, including: Ave Maria • A Mighty Fortress • Hallelujah from *Messiah* • and more.

00221009 ....$9.95

I – DISNEY DUETS
8 songs: Candle on the Water • Colors of the Wind • Cruella de Vil • Hakuna Matata • Someday • A Spoonful of Sugar • Winnie the Pooh • Zip-A-Dee-Doo-Dah.

00290484 ....$12.95

LI – DISNEY MOVIE HITS FOR TWO
9 fun favorites, including: Be Our Guest • Circle of Life • Friend like Me • Under the Sea • A Whole New World • and more.

00292076 ....$14.95

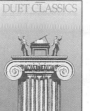
LI – DUET CLASSICS FOR PIANO
8 classical melodies, arranged as piano duets. Includes: Liebestraum (Liszt) • Minuet In G (Beethoven) • Sleeping Beauty Waltz (Tchaikovsky) • and more.

00290172 ....$6.95

LI – GERSHWIN PIANO DUETS
These duet arrangements of 10 Gershwin classics such as "I Got Plenty of Nuttin'," "Summertime," "It Ain't Necessarily So," and "Love Walked In" sound as full and satisfying as the orchestral originals.

00312603 ....$10.95

I – GREAT MOVIE THEMES
8 movie hits, including: Chariots of Fire • Colors of the Wind • The Entertainer • *Forrest Gump – Main Title* • Theme from *Jurassic Park* • Somewhere in Time • Somewhere, My Love • *Star Trek® – The Motion Picture* • and more.

00290494 ....$9.95

UI – LOVE DUETS
7 songs: All I Ask of You • Can You Feel the Love Tonight • Can't Help Falling in Love • Here, There, and Everywhere • Unchained Melody • When I Fall in Love • A Whole New World (Aladdin's Theme).

00290485 ....$8.95

LI – ANDREW LLOYD WEBBER PIANO DUETS
arr. Ann Collins
8 easy piano duets, featuring some of Andrew Lloyd Webber's biggest hits such as: All I Ask of You • Don't Cry for Me Argentina • Memory • I Don't Know How to Love Him.

00290332........................$12.95

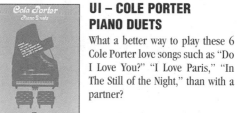
I – MOVIE DUETS
9 songs, including: Chariots of Fire • *The Godfather* (Love Theme) • *Romeo and Juliet* (Love Theme) • Theme from *Schindler's List* • and more.

00292078 ....$9.95

UI – COLE PORTER PIANO DUETS
What a better way to play these 6 Cole Porter love songs such as "Do I Love You?" "I Love Paris," "In The Still of the Night," than with a partner?

00312680........................$9.95

UI – ROCK 'N' ROLL – PIANO DUETS
Ten early rock classics, including: Blue Suede Shoes • Don't Be Cruel • Rock Around the Clock • Shake, Rattle and Roll.

00290171........................$9.95

I – THE SOUND OF MUSIC
9 songs, including: Do-Re-Mi • Edelweiss • My Favorite Things • The Sound of Music • and more.

00290389........................$12.95

GRADING

LI = Lower Intermediate
I = Intermediate
UI = Upper Intermediate

FOR MORE INFORMATION, SEE YOUR LOCAL MUSIC DEALER, OR WRITE TO:

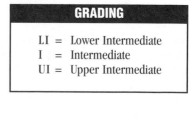
HAL•LEONARD® CORPORATION
7777 W. BLUEMOUND RD. P.O. BOX 13819 MILWAUKEE, WI 53213

www.halleonard.com

The **Piano Duet Play-Along** series gives you the flexibility to rehearse or perform piano duets anytime, anywhere! Play these delightful tunes with a partner, or use the accompanying CDs to play along with either the Secondo or Primo part on your own. The CD is playable on any CD player, and also enhanced so PC and Mac users can adjust the recording to any tempo without changing pitch.

FOR MORE INFORMATION, SEE YOUR LOCAL MUSIC DEALER, OR WRITE TO:

HAL•LEONARD®
CORPORATION
7777 W. BLUEMOUND RD. P.O. BOX 13819 MILWAUKEE, WI 53213

Visit Hal Leonard Online at **www.halleonard.com**

Disney characters and artwork are © Disney Enterprises, Inc.

0709